After three years of teaching and healing, Jesus decided to go to Jerusalem with his twelve disciples. One disciple appears twice in this picture. Which one?
Read this story in Matthew 20:17–19.

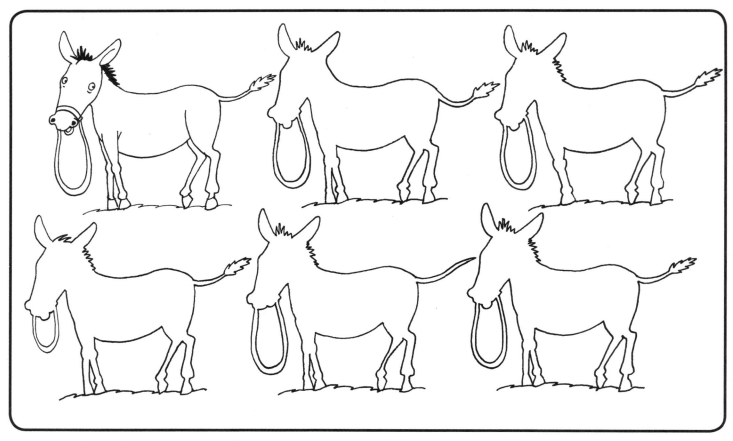

When they were near the city, Jesus told two disciples to borrow a donkey for him.
Which outline fits the finished donkey? Now complete all the donkeys.
You can read this story in Matthew 21:1–7.

The disciples found a donkey and brought it to Jesus. He was going to ride the donkey into Jerusalem. Which box has all the pieces needed to make the donkey?
Read this story in Matthew 21:6–8.

Jesus led his twelve disciples from the Mount of Olives into the great city of Jerusalem.
Can you help him find the correct route?
Read this story in Luke 19:28–38.

What are these people waving as Jesus rides past on his donkey?
Join up the dots to find out.
Read the story in Matthew 21:6–8.

When Jesus entered Jerusalem riding a donkey, the people cheered.
How many matching pairs of people waving palm leaves can you find here?
Read this story in John 12:12–16.

Join up the dots to find out what's missing here.
Who is riding the donkey?
You can find this story in John 12:12–19.

7

When Jesus rode into Jerusalem, many of the people waved palm branches.
What did they throw on the ground? Now draw them in.
Read this story in Luke 19:28–38.

Jesus had come to Jerusalem to celebrate the Feast of Passover.
Which two Jerusalem houses illustrated here are exactly the same?

Here are two houses in Jerusalem (top left).
Which other picture has all the parts needed to make up both houses?

One of Jesus' disciples, Judas Iscariot, was plotting to have Jesus arrested by the Temple guards.
Which of the twelve disciples in the picture is the odd man out? Why?
Read this story in Matthew 26:14–16.

Priests gave Judas 30 silver coins to tell them where they could find Jesus so they could arrest him. Can you find all the deliberate mistakes in this picture?
Read the story in Luke 22:1–6.

The artist has drawn three matching pairs of Roman coins.
Can you find all the pairs?
Read about the money that Judas Iscariot was paid in Matthew 26:14–16.

Here are two priests from the Temple in Jerusalem. They are plotting how to arrest Jesus. Can you find ten scrolls hidden in the picture?
Read this story in Matthew 26:3–4.

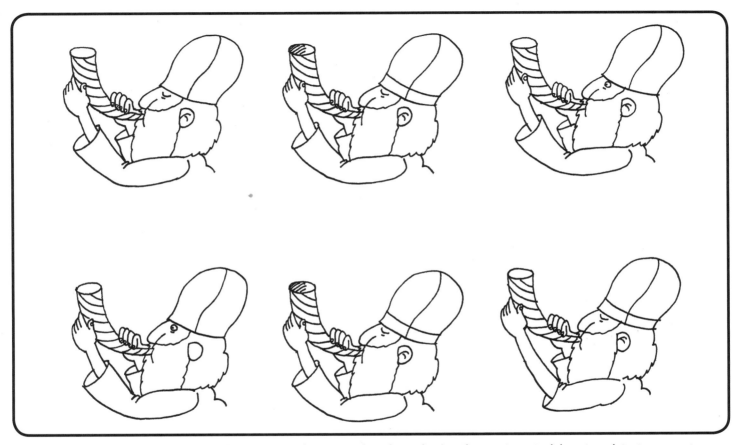

Some of the priests hated Jesus and wanted to hurt him. This priest is blowing his trumpet. It is made from a ram's horn. Find two pictures that are exactly the same.
Read about the priests' plot in Matthew 26:3–4.

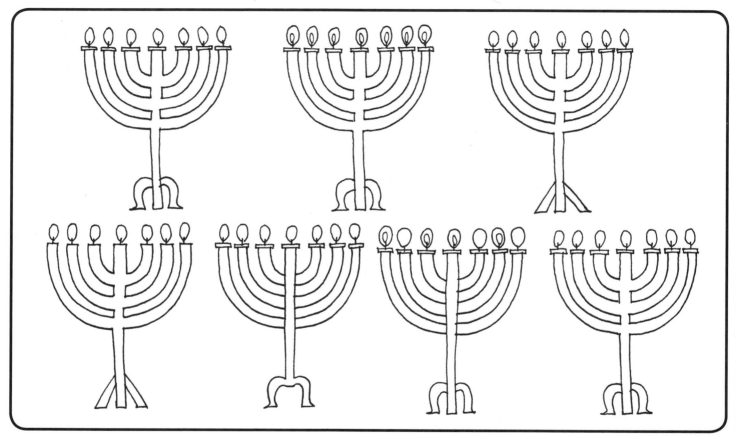

Inside the Jerusalem Temple stood a beautiful, gold seven-branched candlestick.
The artist has drawn it seven times. Which two pictures are exactly the same?
Read about the Temple priests' plot against Jesus in Luke 22:1–6.

When he was in Jerusalem, Jesus went to the Temple to pray.
But what is Jesus doing here? Join up the dots to find out.
Now read John 2:13–22 to find the complete story.

How many differences can you find between these two pictures?
What is Jesus doing here, in the Jerusalem Temple?
Read the whole story in Mark 11:15–17.

This man is carrying fruit to sell at the market in Jerusalem.
Can you discover ten differences between the reflected drawings?

Jesus and his disciples were having a special meal to celebrate the Festival of Passover.
This woman is bringing water for the feast. Which outline matches the finished drawing?
Read about the feast in Luke 22:7–12.

Jesus ate the special supper with his twelve disciples in the upper room of a house in Jerusalem.
Fill in this picture of the meal with your crayons or felt-tips.
Read about this meal in Matthew 26:26.

What is Jesus doing here?
Is he washing something – or someone?
Read John 13:1–17 to find out, then complete the picture.

22

During their meal, Jesus shared a cup of wine with his disciples.
Here are five drawings of wine cups and a wine jar. Which two are identical?
Read Matthew 26:27–29 to find out what Jesus said as he shared the wine.

Here is the artist's picture of Jesus and his friends eating and drinking at the Last Supper.
Copy the picture in the empty box. Now finish it with felt-tips or crayons.
Read about this meal in Matthew 26:17–30.

At the Last Supper, Jesus shared wine with his disciples.
How many drinking cups can you find here? Are there more than fifteen?
Read this story in Matthew 26:27–29.

At the Last Supper in Jerusalem, Jesus shared wine with his disciples. It was made from grapes.
Here are five bunches of grapes. Which two are exactly the same?
Read what Jesus told his disciples about the vine and its branches in John 15:1–17.

After supper, Jesus led his disciples to the Garden of Gethsemane, outside Jerusalem.
Jesus prayed, but his disciples fell asleep. How many mistakes can you find in this picture?
Read this story in Matthew 26:40–45.

The guards were searching for Jesus so they could arrest him.
Which path leads the soldiers to Jesus?
Read this story in Matthew 26:45–47.

The guards soon found Jesus and arrested him. Who is the man staring at Jesus?
Write in his name. Finish the picture with felt-tips or crayons.
Read this story in Matthew 26:47–56.

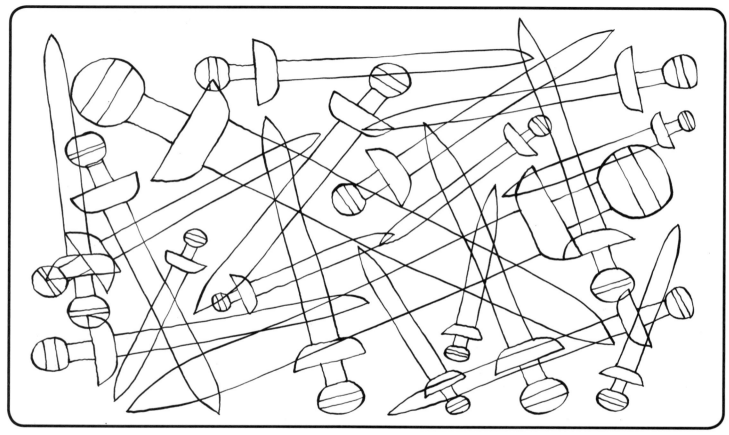

One of Jesus' disciples drew his sword and cut off the ear of one of the Temple soldiers.
What was the disciple's name? *Read John 18:1–11 to find out.*
How many swords can you find in this drawing?

Jesus was arrested by the soldiers in the garden. What is the disciple on the left doing?
You can read this story in Matthew 26:47–56.
Now finish the picture with felt-tips or crayons.

Here are some of the Roman soldiers who guarded Jesus. The artist has finished one picture. Which outline completely fits the finished soldier? Now finish drawing the other figures. *Read what the soldiers did to Jesus in Mark 15:16–20.*

When the soldiers arrested Jesus, Peter said he didn't know his Master.
Why was he sad when he heard a cockerel crow? *Read Mark 14:66–72 to find out.*
How many differences can you find between the two pictures?

A cockerel crowed after Peter pretended he wasn't one of Jesus' disciples.
Which box has all the pieces needed to make up the cockerel in the first box?
Read this story in John 18:15–18, 25–27.

After Jesus had been arrested, he was taken before the Jewish high priest, who was called Caiaphas. *You can read what happened in Matthew 26:57.* Finish this picture with crayons or felt-tips.

Something is missing in this picture of the high priest, Caiaphas.
Why is he looking so stern? *Read the story in Matthew 26:57–66.*
Now complete the drawing, adding any missing people.

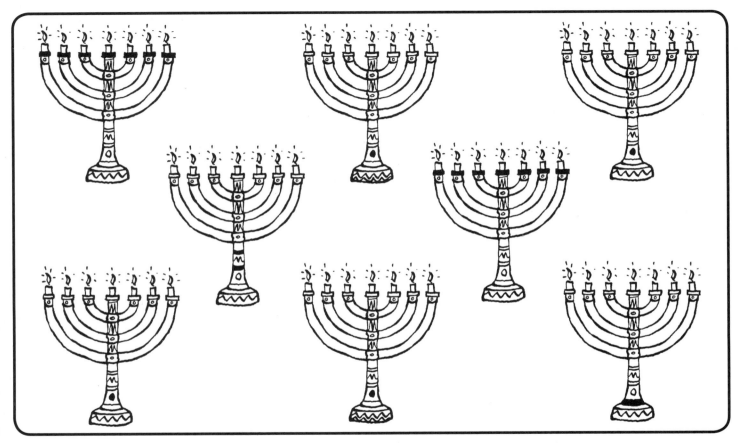

Caiaphas was high priest of the wonderful Temple in Jerusalem.
Inside the Temple was a seven-branched candlestick, made of gold.
Can you find three identical pairs of candlesticks here?

The artist has drawn Caiaphas the high priest and three other priests in outline.
Complete all three drawings.
Read what happened when Jesus was taken to the high priest, in Matthew 26:57–68.

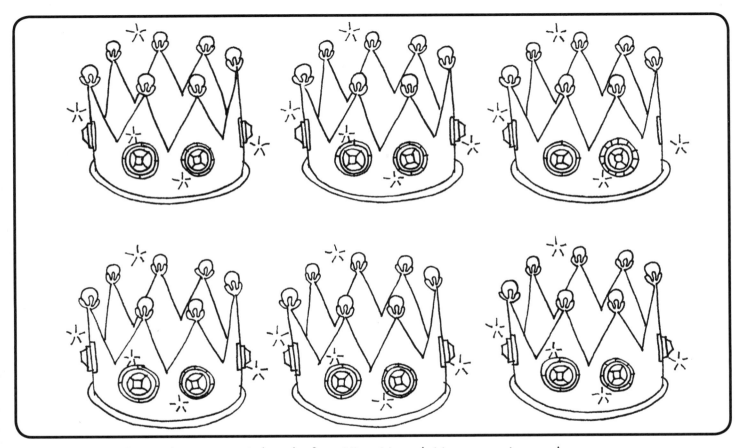

Later, Jesus was taken before King Herod. Here are six royal crowns.
Which crown is the odd one out? *Read about Herod meeting Jesus in Luke 23:6–12.*
Why was Herod pleased to meet Jesus?

Finally, Jesus was taken before the Roman governor. Join up the dots to find him.
What was the governor's name? *Find out in John 18:28–38.*

In this picture of Pontius Pilate sitting in judgment, the prisoner is missing.
Read Matthew 27:11–26 then complete the picture.

Pilate's wife had a dream about Jesus. She sent a messenger to Pilate to tell him Jesus was innocent. Which route takes the messenger to Pilate in his judge's chair? *Read this story in Matthew 27:19.*

Pilate washed his hands to show he didn't want to take the blame for putting Jesus to death.
Can you find six bowls hidden in this picture?
Read this story in Matthew 27:11–26.

Pilate washed his hands before he judged Jesus.
Read this story in Matthew 27:24–26. Now fill in Pilate's speech bubble.
Why did Pilate wash his hands?

The Roman soldiers treated Jesus very cruelly.
Which of these four soldiers is the odd one out? Why?
Read Matthew 27:27–31 to discover what the soldiers did.

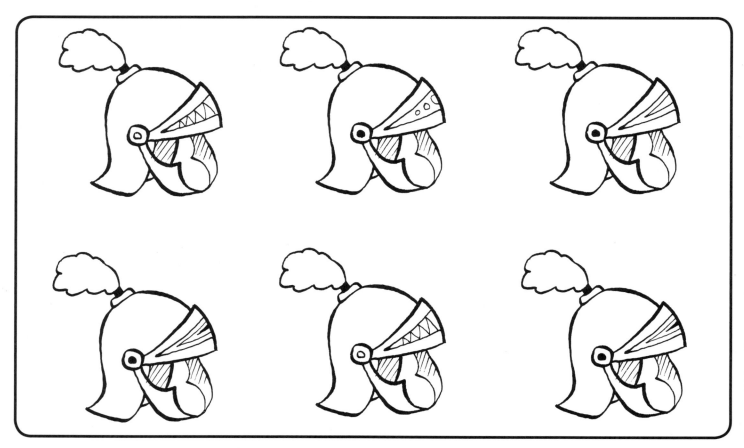

Roman soldiers took Jesus outside the walls of Jerusalem.
There are two matching pairs of Roman helmets. Can you find them?
Read this part of the story in Matthew 27:27–38.

The Roman soldiers took Jesus to a place called Skull Hill, and put him on a cross to die.
He was between two thieves. *You can read about this in Luke 23:33.*
What did the Roman officer say when Jesus died? Complete the picture with felt-tips.

47

Jesus was put to death on a cross. What did he say just before he died?
Find the words in John 19:30. Now fill in the speech bubble.
Who are the women kneeling on the ground?

Here are six pictures from the story of Jesus dying on the cross.
Can you number them in the correct order?
Read Matthew chapters 26 and 27 to help you.

Judas gave back the thirty silver coins he was paid to lead the soldiers to arrest Jesus.
Can you find ten coins hidden in this picture? Who are the other men?
Look up this story in Matthew 27:1–10.

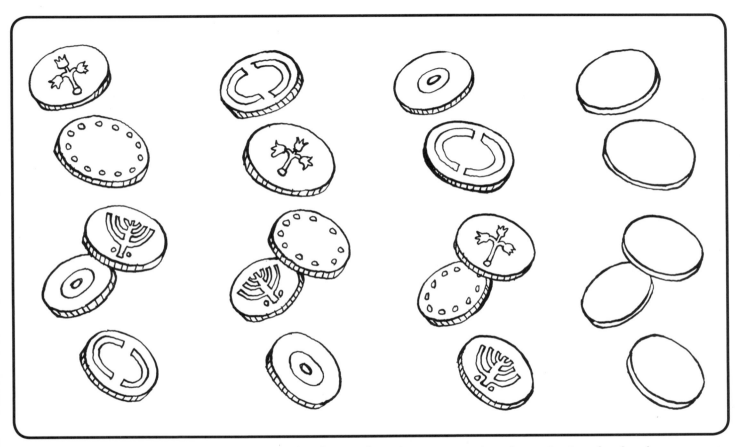

Judas threw silver coins on the floor when he returned to the priests who had plotted against Jesus. The pattern on these coins moves downwards. Can you complete the pattern on the last row of coins? *Read this story in Matthew 27:1–10.*

After Jesus died on the cross, he was buried in a cave. Roman soldiers stood guard at the door. It was made from a great, round stone. *You can read about this in Matthew 27:65.* Finish off the picture with crayons or felt-tips.

Roman soldiers were put on guard outside Jesus' tomb.
The artist has finished one picture: complete the other two pictures of Roman soldiers.
Read Matthew 27:62–66.

Very early in the morning, three women went to visit Jesus' tomb.
They got a big surprise. Join up the dots to find out why.
Now read the whole story in Luke 24:1–12.

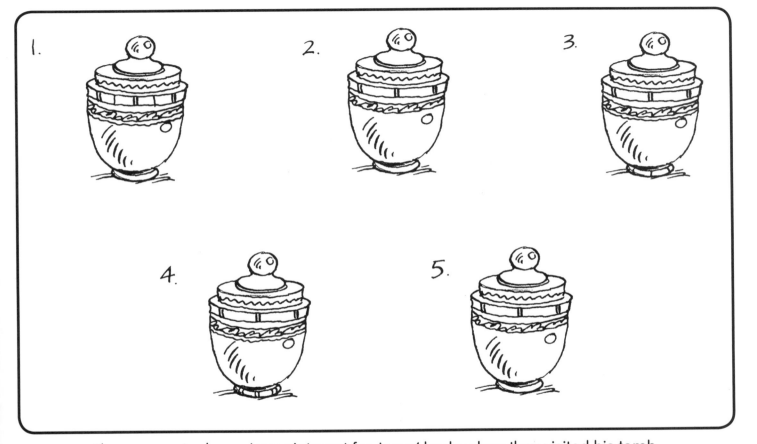

The women took precious ointment for Jesus' body when they visited his tomb.
Here are five drawings of the jar of ointment. Which two are exactly the same?
You can read about the women's visit in Luke 23:55 – 24:2.

The women discovered Jesus' tomb was empty.
Can you find all the differences between these two pictures of the empty tomb?
Read the story in Luke 24:1–12. Who spoke to the women when they visited the tomb?

Jesus' friend Mary was very sad when she found Jesus' tomb was empty.
She thought someone had stolen his body. Can you find thirteen butterflies hidden in this picture?
Read the story of Mary visiting Jesus' tomb in John 20:11–18.

Mary stood outside Jesus' empty tomb. She met someone she thought was the gardener.
Join up the dots to discover who it really was.
Read this story in John 20:11–18.

The tomb was empty because Jesus had risen from the dead. He appeared to his disciples when they were in a locked room. Can you find ten keys hidden in this picture?
Read this story in John 20:19–20.

Meanwhile, two of Jesus' friends left Jerusalem and walked sadly home to their village. They thought Jesus was still dead. But someone joined them on the road? Who? *Read Luke 24:13–35 to find out.* Now complete the drawing.

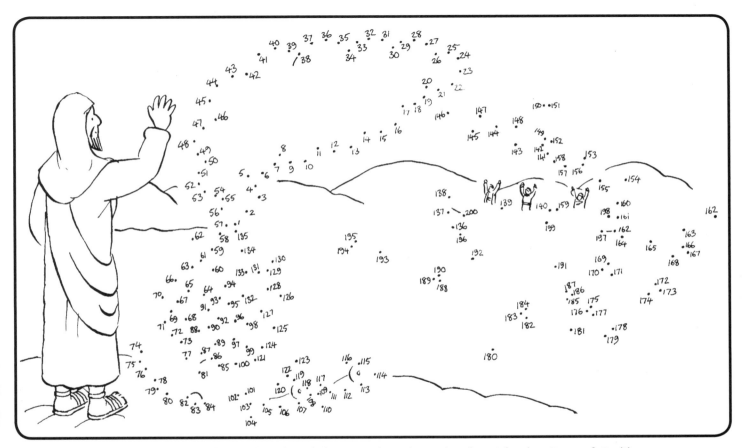

After Jesus rose from the dead, he met his disciples beside the Sea of Galilee.
Join up the dots to discover what's happening here.
Now read this story in John 21:1–14.

Forty days after he rose from the dead, Jesus returned to his Father.
Read Luke 24:50–53 to get the whole story.
Finish this illustration, using crayons or felt-tips.

After Jesus returned to his Father, the disciples returned to Jerusalem. They were in a room together when tongues of fire appeared on their heads. *Read this story in Acts 2:1–4.* Which group of disciples here is the odd one out?

After Jesus returned to heaven, his disciples started to tell other people that he had risen from the dead. Join up the dots to find out what Jesus' friend Peter is doing here.
Now read this story in Acts 3:1–10.